Charles Patrick Neill

Daniel Raymond, an early chapter in the history of economic theory in the United States

Fifteenth Series

Charles Patrick Neill

Daniel Raymond, an early chapter in the history of economic theory in the United States
Fifteenth Series

ISBN/EAN: 9783337277901

Printed in Europe, USA, Canada, Australia, Japan

Cover: Foto ©Suzi / pixelio.de

More available books at **www.hansebooks.com**

DANIEL RAYMOND

An Early Chapter in the History of Economic Theory in the United States.

JOHNS HOPKINS UNIVERSITY STUDIES

IN

HISTORICAL AND POLITICAL SCIENCE

HERBERT B. ADAMS, Editor

History is past Politics and Politics are present History.—*Freeman*.

FIFTEENTH SERIES

VI

DANIEL RAYMOND

An Early Chapter in the History of Economic Theory
in the United States

By CHARLES PATRICK NEILL, A. M.

Instructor in Economics in the Catholic University of America.

BALTIMORE

THE JOHNS HOPKINS PRESS

PUBLISHED MONTHLY

June, 1897

GUGGENHEIMER, WEIL & CO., PRINTERS,
BALTIMORE.

TABLE OF CONTENTS.

DANIEL RAYMOND

AN EARLY CHAPTER IN THE HISTORY OF ECONOMIC THEORY IN THE UNITED STATES.

INTRODUCTION.

The net result of a study of the history of economic science in the United States during the first century of our national existence has been summed up thus:

"Not only has no American school of writers on political economy been established, if we except that which we are about to notice (Henry C. Carey and his several disciples), but no recognized contribution to the development of the science can be pointed out in any way comparable to those made by the French writers, or to those which the Germans are now making."[1]

"The general result then to which, as we believe, a sober examination of the case must lead any candid inquirer, is that the United States have, thus far, done nothing towards developing the theory of political economy, notwithstanding their vast and immediate interest in its practical applications."[2]

Despite this foreshadowing of negative results, the present study was begun in the belief that a further investigation into the history of economic science in the United States would not be without scientific interest. Had this country produced no economic writers at all, the causes of such barrenness would have invited inquiry; and if we have produced writers, and these have been without influence on the development of the science, the why of this is also worthy of study.

The results of the present study would seem to indicate that perhaps American writers have exerted an influence upon

---

[1]North American Review, January 1876, p. 137. Dunbar, Economic Science in the United States, 1776-1876.
[2]*Ibid.*, p. 140.

the development of the science to an extent that has not heretofore been conceded.

The general history of economic science has been divided into the fragmentary period, in which isolated discussions of economic topics are found scattered about in the writings of thinkers in other fields; the period of monographs and empirical systems; the constructive period, in which systematic treatises appear, essaying the presentation of a complete science; and the critical or analytical period.[1] Although the appearance of the United States in the family of nations was subsequent to the beginning of this third period—or, perhaps, coincident with it— the history of the development of the science here, or rather of its development at the hands of American writers, reproduces the phases marked in its general history.

The year 1820 may be said to have ushered in the third period in the United States,[2] with the publication of a treatise on political economy from the pen of Daniel Raymond, of the Baltimore bar; and it is of this writer and his work that the present monograph purposes to treat.

The importance of Raymond's work is not alone in that it is the first systematic treatise on economics from the pen of an American, but also in that it shows the influence of American conditions, and in consequence presents a theory of political economy opposed at all points to the prevailing system as developed by the dominant school of Adam Smith.

Before dealing with the work of Raymond, it may not be amiss to sketch in brief the condition of economic thought in this country during the period preceding his appearance as an economist.

---

[1] Cossa, Introduction to Study of Political Economy.

[2] "Down to the year 1820 no American produced any treatise on political economy which the world has cared to remember." *N. A. Rev.*, January, 1876, p. 134.

"There is no American treatise on the subject, ———. The only American book that has the semblance of a treatise on political economy is Hamilton's reports as Secretary of the Treasury." Raymond, 1st ed. (1820), p. 5.

CHAPTER I.

EARLY ECONOMIC THOUGHT IN THE UNITED STATES.

In a new country, as was the United States of a century ago, with meager facilities for education—and that education dominated largely by the classics—with crude social conditions, and, in consequence, little leisure or inclination on the part of the people for abstract study or speculative thought, one does not expect to find any extensive knowledge of the principles of the new science of economics, or any very profound interest taken in its study. If this knowledge or interest were to be looked for anywhere, it would be amongst the statesmen of the day; for politics had very largely absorbed the best intelligence of the time, the up-building on permanent lines of the new political structure demanded attention to basic principles and not shifting expedients, and the most important and most fiercely contested political issues of the day were distinctively economic. But even the architects of our political and industrial system do not seem to have depended much on the light that a study of the rising science might have afforded them, nor do they seem to have been much influenced by arguments drawn from it.

Franklin had indeed in his speculations discussed numerous economic topics, and by some of his reviewers he has been reconstructed into an economist worthy of his time;[1]

---

[1] Wetzel, Benjamin Franklin as an Economist, J. H. U. Studies.

but a less admiring critic has given the weight of his authority to the proposition that Franklin "not only did not advance the growth of economic science, but he seems not
even to have mastered it as it was already developed."[1]
From Franklin to Alexander Hamilton no public man seems
to have displayed any grasp of economic principles sufficient to have made him worthy of note on that account.[2]
Hamilton in this respect stands out in bold relief amongst
his fellows, and yet his mastery of the best economic thought
of his day, and his skill in expounding and applying its principles, does not seem to have enabled him to win over ready
assent to his measures. His plan for a national bank as a
fiscal aid to the government and a regulator of the currency
was made possible rather through a "deal" of the sort termed
"practical politics," than as a result of economic thinking;
and his protective measures only became a national policy
long years after his report on manufactures, and then only
as the result of new developments, and not in direct consequence of his writings. The political rather than the economic bearing of measures was the influence that determined legislation. Were they centralizing or decentraliz-
ing?—this was the aspect that appealed to the men who were
fashioning the new republic. With their minds haunted by
this all important question, they were little likely to be influenced by the principles of Adam Smith's new science.
It might be useful as lending added support to theories already accepted on other grounds; but it would scarcely win
assent to its principles from those to whose minds political
considerations had already given an opposite trend.

The study of economic science made headway slowly at
first. An American edition of Adam Smith had made its
appearance at Philadelphia as early as 1789.[3] Two decades
seem to have elapsed before there was a growth of interest in

---

[1] Prof. Dunbar in *N. A. Rev.*, January, 1876, p. 130.
[2] *Ibid.*, p. 131.
[3] Catalogue of Baltimore Athenaeum Library, 1827.

the science sufficient to warrant another edition. A second reprint appeared from Hartford in 1811, and a third from the same place in 1818. Interest seems to have been awakening about this time, for in 1819, only two years after its appearance in England, Ricardo's "Principles" was reprinted at Georgetown, and a translation of Say appeared from the same place in 1821, and was quickly followed by a second edition.[1] Cossa implies[2] that these reprints were partly, if not largely, for use in the schools, but at this time political economy had found place in college curricula only in a few instances, and not by any means to an extent to have called for such a multiplication of text books. It is more likely that the rising sentiment for a protective system was attracting interest to economic principles; and that the advocates of free trade were becoming zealous not only in the study of their master, but also in placing within easy reach of their dissenting brethren authentic copies of the creed of true believers.[3]

Jefferson, who had been exposed to the infection in France, was very much interested in the science of political economy, and very earnestly bent on stimulating the study of it among his fellow-citizens. Through his efforts "A Treatise on Political Economy," by "Count Destutt Tracy, member of the Senate and Institute of France, and of the American Philosophical Society," was translated from the original French manuscript, and published at Georgetown in 1817. Jefferson regarded this author as "the ablest writer living on intellectual subjects;" and when the book issued from the press, it was prefaced by a letter from Jefferson, in which he indulges the hope that its merits will win for it a "place in the hands of every reader in our country," and

---

[1] Carey, Biographical Sketches, p. 9.

[2] Introduction to the Study of Political Economy, p. 466.

[3] In marked contrast to the inactivity of their opponents, the free traders were at this time active propagandists. *Cf.* Mathew Carey, Biographical Sketches.

says that it is his "hearty prayer" that it may be made the elementary book of instruction in the science.[1]

After its publication, John Adams wrote of this book: "Upon the subject of political economy at large, I know of nothing better."[2] Yet notwithstanding that the work could elicit such high praise, Jefferson had been for five years trying to secure a publisher for it before his efforts bore fruit.[3] The book dealt with abstract principles, and was metaphysical; it was consequently of little avail as a weapon for political strife; and it was this latter aspect of a work on political economy that determined its popularity.

Jefferson's efforts to spread a knowledge of economic principles among his compeers were not, on the whole, encouraging; and from some of his letters we may glean his opinion of the condition of the science in this country in his day.[4]

---

[1] It was originally intended that this work should be first published in this country, on account of the author's fear of incurring the displeasure of Napoleon should it come to his notice. Though Jefferson arranged for its publication here, his name was not to be publicly connected with the work, as the author was prepared to deny its authenticity, in case it should come to the notice of Napoleon. But before a publisher could be secured here, Napoleon had been deposed, and the work appeared in France before it issued from the press here. Jefferson's Works, edited by H. A. Washington, Vol. VI., p. 568; Vol. VII., p. 39.

[2] A's works, Vol. X., p. 385.

[3] J's works, Vols. VI.-VII.

[4] To Dupont de Nemours, Feb. 28, 1815:

"With sufficient means in the hands of our citizens, and sufficient will to bestow them on the government, we are floundering in expedients equally unproductive and ruinous; and proving how little are understood here those sound principles of political economy first developed by the economists, since commented and dilated by Smith, Say, yourself, and the luminous reviewer of Montesquieu. I have been endeavoring to get the able paper on the subject, which you addressed to me July, 1810, and enlarged in a copy received the last year, translated and printed here in order to draw the attention of our citizens to the subject; but have not as yet succeeded. Our printers are enterprising only in novels and light reading. The readers of works of science, although in considerable numbers, are so sparse in their situations, that such works are of slow circulation. But I shall persevere." *Ibid.*, Vol. VI., p. 429.

During the first thirty years, then, of our national existence little attention seems to have been bestowed upon the
study of economic science.   An interest in it begins to show
itself in the closing years of the first quarter of the present
century.   The philosophy of that day had everywhere taken
for its shibboleth "Liberty, Freedom;" and in a country such
as ours, which had so recently freed itself—after much sacri-
fice—from being too much and too capriciously governed,
which had, within the memory of citizens not yet old, been
regarded merely as territory to be exploited as best suited
the interests of the classes controlling the "home government," it was only natural that the philosophy of individualism should find a congenial soil, and that the colonists, become citizens, should look askance at government, watch
with jealous eye its every expansion of function, plan to
hedge it about with restraints, and take kindly to the doctrine of *laissez faire*.   Accordingly, then, when an interest
in economic science begins to awaken here, there is a pre-
disposition to accept the system of Adam Smith, to cling to
it as the teaching of wisdom, and to erect it into the creed
of orthodoxy.   Such was the status of economic science in
the United States when the first American treatise on the
subject appeared.

To Dupont, May 15, 1815:
    "The newspapers tell us that you are arrived in the United States.
. . . . . . You will now be a witness to our deplorable ignorance in finance and political economy generally. I mentioned in my
letter of February that I was endeavoring to get your memoir on
that subject printed. I have not yet succeeded." Vol VI., p. 458.
To M. Carrea de Serra, Dec. 27, 1814:
    "I have received a letter from Mr. Say, in which he expresses a
thought of removing to this country. . . . '. Mr. Say will be
surprised to find, that forty years after the development of sound
financial principles by Adam Smith and the economists, and a dozen
years after he has given them to us in a corrected, dense, and lucid
form, there should be so much ignorance of them in our country;
that . . . we are trusting to tricks of jugglers on the cards, to
the illusions of banking schemes for the resources of the war, and
for the cure of colic to the inflation of more wind." Vol. VI., p. 406.

CHAPTER II.

Daniel Raymond and His Work.

Daniel Raymond (1786-1849) was a native of Connecticut. He prepared himself for the bar in the law school of Tapping Reeve, at Litchfield, Conn.,[1] and in 1814 appears as a member of the bar of Baltimore.[2] He had brought with him to the land of his adoption the New England hatred of its peculiar institution, and in 1819 he came before the public in a pamphlet on the "Missouri Question."

In 1820 he essayed a more ambitious role, and gave to the public his "Thoughts on Political Economy" (Vol. I., pp. 470). This was the first systematic treatise on the subject to be written by an American,[3] and it may not be without interest to know what led to his taking up the subject. Raymond's own explanation is frank, and sufficiently modest. The public permitted him many moments of leisure in his profession; poring over "musty law books" had grown a weariness of the flesh; idleness too was irksome; and for mere diversion he set about putting on paper his thoughts on political economy.[4] As he wrote his subject developed

[1] Federal Gazette and Balto. Daily Advertiser, Dec. 26, 1823.

[2] Records of the Superior Court, Baltimore.

[3] Supra, p. 2.

[4] "The following sheets were written to please myself—my principal object in writing them, was employment. The public has not seen fit to give me constant employment in my profession, otherwise this book had never been written. I had read musty law books till I was tired. Idleness was irksome, and I sought relief in putting on paper some of my thoughts on political economy. If the public shall think this a sufficient justification for writing a book, it is well; if not, I cannot help it. I have no other to offer.

"As to my inducement for publishing it, I know not what to say. . . . . . The best excuse I can allege for publishing is, that it pleased me so to do, and one feels a sort of satisfaction in doing as he pleases, without consulting any one." Preface to 1st ed. p. 1.

in his mind beyond anticipated proportions;[1] and then, to please his whim, he put his notes into the hands of the printer. He styles his book "Thoughts on Political Economy;" he does not send it out as a "general treatise on political economy;" he modestly professes his inability to write such a treatise; and the only merit to which he lays claim is that of a pioneer in the attempt to shake off the domination of "foreign theories and systems of political economy," and develop in their stead a system suited to America."[2]

Raymond's system was strongly antagonistic to the prevailing individualistic philosophy; it leaned to governmental interference in opposition to *laissez faire,* stood for protective tariffs, decried banks and paper money, and hurled anathemas at slavery as an economic evil, an abomination before the Lord, and a curse alike upon enslavers and enslaved. It thus touched upon sorely vexed questions of the day over which the fiercest political contests were being waged; and in consequence it was only to be expected that it would win enthusiastic admirers on the one hand, and harsh critics on the other—each equally biased and one-sided in their respective estimates of the work. Discriminating judgment was hardly to be looked for.

---

[1] "At the time this book was commenced, I had no expectation of writing more than a small pamphlet, and of this I scarcely anticipated a publication. As I have said before, I wrote rather for my own amusement and instruction, than for the public; but as I progressed the subject became more interesting—new views and ideas suggested themselves—and I pressed onward until it has grown to a volume." P. 469.

[2] "I am far from supposing that this book can properly be demoninated a general treatise on political economy. I do not profess to be able to write such a book. All I say is that it is a more general treatise than any that has to my knowledge been written in our country, and all the merit I claim for it, on this account, is, that of having made an humble effort to break loose from the fetters of foreign authority; from foreign theories and systems of political economy, which from the dissimilarity in the nature of the governments, renders them altogether unsuited to our country." Preface to 1st ed., pp. V.-VI.

The *North American Review*[1] devoted twenty-three pages of its space to Raymond's work. The reviewer[2] is a free trader and worships at the shrine of Adam Smith. As a heretic Raymond calls out his severest condemnation. The criticism is caustic,[3] and the reviewer has on his "learned sock." He essays to write profoundly, but gets no farther than irrelevant quibbles and pedantic dialectic; he misses the real importance of Raymond's work, its significant characteristic escapes him entirely.

The *National Recorder*, of Philadelphia, a journal professing to speak authoritatively on the subject of political economy, adds the weight of its disapproval. It deprecates the intrusion into the economic field of a man bred to the profession of the law, and seems to think the shoemaker would best stick to his last.[4]

The *National Gazette*,[5] of Philadelphia, concedes to Raymond "a nice discernment and a marked capacity for the investigations in which he has engaged;" but it cannot forgive him for "an extravagant disparagement of the great lights of the science which he treats, and an overweening confidence in the superior justness of his own perceptions, and the superior acuteness and solidity of his own reasonings,"—a criticism to which Raymond had undeniably laid himself open.

---

[1] April, 1821, Vol. XII.

[2] F. C. Gray, LL. D., an attorney of Salem, Mass.

[3] "It would have been no derogation from the merit of this work had it appeared before the public with humbler pretensions. It . . . . lays claim to complete originality. . . . . . . The science of political economy is so little an object of popular attention, and has really made so much progress unobserved by the community, that the student on first engaging in it, is apt to be astonished at the result of his inquiries, and to fancy that what is so new to him must be new to others. But in this as in other pursuits, the boast of superior wisdom does not arise from an excess of knowledge so often as from a want of it."

[4] *Cf.* Fed. Gaz. and Balto. Daily Ad., January 31, 1821.

[5] January 12, 1821.

The prophet, however, was not without honor in his own country, which, in this instance, is interpreted to mean Baltimore.

Niles' Register,[1] of Baltimore, strongly protectionist, pronounces favorable judgment upon the work, and "can recommend it to the consideration of those who are desirous of information upon this important subject, as well worthy of attentive perusal."

The *Federal Gazette and Baltimore Daily Advertiser*[2] thinks the work "evinces considerable talent, deep research, and attentive and judicious consideration of the subject," and that it is "highly honorable to the author, and worthy of the attention of our fellow-citizens." The *Gazette*, with commendable local pride, also takes up the cudgel in defense of its fellow-townsman against the attacks of its Philadelphia contemporaries, which, it alleges, are inspired by hatred of everything that comes out of Baltimore.

Farther from home Raymond's work found even more enthusiastic admirers,—in the protectionist camp. The *Patron of Industry*, a journal published in New York, wearied, probably, by "the servile homage to the theories put forth in the name of political economy in Europe," waxed enthusiastic and hailed the work as an honor to the author, his subject, and his country.[3]

---

[1] Dec. 16, 1820.

[2] Dec. 13, 1820.

[3] "We took up this work in the anxious hope that the author, whether right or wrong in his system, was in point of talents worthy to be the author of the first formal treatise upon the subject of Political Economy on this side of the Atlantic, and that he had sufficient courage to take the field against the spirit of servile homage to the theories put forth in the name of political economy in Europe from the period of the economists down to the present day.

"The perusal of the work did not disappoint us in these particulars. The writer has given evidence, not only of talents adequate to his undertaking, but of a disposition to employ the powers of his mind in simplifying and rendering clear and perspicuous what others have treated obscurely, and rendered inconsistent and incomprehensible. The book cannot only be read without fatigue, but it can be under-

Frederick Beasley, provost of the University of Pennsylvania, wrote encouragingly to the author, to express the gratification that he as an American felt in a countryman who displayed "such just and profound comprehension of his subject."[1]

John Adams, from his retreat at Montizello, writes that he regards it as the best work that has appeared on political economy, and "a proud monument of American literature;" and he purposes constituting himself its propagandist.[2]

Mathew Carey, then bearing the heat and burden of the battle for protection, and delighted to find a brother pro-

stood. The writer has treated his subject far more scientifically than his predecessors, not merely in his divisions and definitions, but also in his precision in the use of words, and in the employment of technical terms and phrases.

"As to the doctrines taught in this book they are to a considerable extent new; and in most part they differ from the old ones to which they stand opposed, we think very much as nature differs from art, truth from fiction and light from darkness. There are several fundamental points, concerning which the various writers in political economy have been most bewildered and inconsistent, which by starting right and reasoning right, he appears to us to have extricated from the confusion by which they have so long been embarrassed. Such are the nature of national wealth—labor, productive and unproductive, standard of value, source and cause of national wealth, mercantile system, &c., &c. We have no hesitation in saying, that we think he has thrown more light on several of these questions than all the other writers who have meddled with them.

"We should have liked his preface well enough if it had not been in the front of his book. It does not fairly introduce the reader to the acute, logical, and philosophic mind which is spread over the succeeding pages. We know nothing of the author; but we hail his work as an honor to himself, his country and his subject."

[1]"I have read it with close attention, and I cannot refrain from expressing to you the pleasure it has given me. Amidst the false tastes and crude productions of the times, it is a real gratification to an American, who has at heart the literary reputation of his country, to find a writer who displays such clear views, just and profound comprehension of his subject, and such neatness and perspicuity of style." *Cf.* preface to Raymond's 4th ed.

[2]"Although reading is almost an intolerable imposition upon my eyes, yet I have read this volume through, and have been richly re-

tectionist, pronounces "Raymond's political economy a work far superior" to either Smith's Wealth of Nations or Say's Political Economy.[1]   So impressed was Carey with Raymond's work, that, "in a moment of enthusiasm," he made an offer of $500 a year to the University of Maryland,[2] for

---

warded for my pains, by the pleasure and instruction I have received. . . . . I have never read any work upon political economy with more satisfaction. It is a rich addition to my library, or what is of infinitely more importance, a proud monument of American literature. . . . . You have indeed cracked the shell of political economy and extracted the purest oil from the nut. I shall warmly recommend it to the perusal of every man of letters that I see." *Ibid.*

[1]Biographical Sketches. p. 9.

[2]It is to be regretted that the whole history of this episode can not be given. The records of the University have been destroyed by fire, but the following extracts from Carey's Biographical Sketches give the external history:

"In this year I displayed a degree of quixotism, that might have cost me dear, but I fortunately escaped. Daniel Raymond, Esq., of Baltimore, had just published his "Political Economy," a valuable work, containing more sound practical truths than I had ever seen in any book on the subject. I was delighted with the work and, in a moment of enthusiasm, it struck me that a course of lectures on the subject, to be delivered by Mr. Raymond, would have a most salutary effect. Accordingly, I gave a pledge to the University of Maryland, to pay five hundred dollars a year towards the expense of a professorship of political economy in that institution. To the discredit of the faculty be it said that they did not condescend to reply to me. They, however, declined to make any additional provision on the subject, and the sum I proposed not being sufficient to induce Mr. Raymond to abandon his practice the project fell to the ground. My reason for applying to the University of Maryland, was that Mr. Raymond lived in Baltimore, and I was determined that he alone should be the lecturer, as I would then be sure not to throw away my money to promulgate pernicious doctrines."

"Philadelphia, January 12, 1822.

"Know all men by these presents, that I do hereby bind myself to pay to the University of Maryland, the sum of 500 dollars, as one year's salary for a professor of political economy, and also to continue the subscription, unless I shall give six month's previous notice of my determination to discontinue the same.

(Signed)   Mathew Carey."

the purpose of endowing a professorship of political economy to be filled by Raymond.   But this offer, opening up a

---

Letter from Carey to Raymond:

"Philadelphia, January 12, 1822.

"I have fully made up my mind to establish the professorship as stated in my last letter, provided it can be done for 500 dollars per annum.   I shall pay one-half of the first year's salary, on the delivery of the first lecture, and the other half on the completion of the course.

"Should I at any time determine to withdraw from the undertaking, I shall regard myself at liberty to do so, on giving six months' previous notice. *But it is highly probable that I shall continue it as long as I live; and indeed make provision for it at my death.*   You are at liberty to make the necessary inquiries of the president of the university.   As for your fitness for the situation, it cannot be questioned.   I regard you as peculiarly qualified for it."

From Raymond to Carey:

"Baltimore, January 18, 1822.

"Your letter, stating the liberal endowment you propose to make towards the establishment of a professorship of political economy for the University of Maryland, has been received and laid before the board of regents, who will, no doubt, duly appreciate your munificence and communicate with you further on the subject.

As regards myself, although it may not be in my power to co-operate with you in carrying your patriotic design into effect, yet I shall ever feel a grateful sense of your kindness and liberality."

From Carey to Raymond:

"Philadelphia, January 19, 1822.

"I feel much uneasiness at the receipt of your letter, lest you should not undertake the professorship in question.   My views were directed to Maryland, entirely in consequence of the confidence I felt that the choice would fall on you, and of my approbation of the principles of political economy you have so ably advocated.

"In the event of your declining, or not being elected, the choice may fall on some person who may preach unsound doctrines, pernicious to the happiness of our citizens, and to the prosperity of the nation.   In this case, I should devote my money to a purpose diametrically opposite to my intentions.   Against this I here enter my protest.   The foreign world furnishes us with apostles sufficient to preach those pestiferous doctrines whose operation has blasted the energies of the nation, and effectively rendered her a colony to the manufacturing nations of the old world.   We have no need to hire them here to accomplish this baleful purpose."   Biographical Sketches, pp. 93-96.

vista of possibilities, came to naught. It is possible that Raymond's chapter on slavery was a factor in determining the outcome.

Despite the warm commendation the work excited in some quarters, it was not able to "command the attention of the generality of readers." It was offered to the public in an edition of hardly more than seven hundred and fifty copies, and of this number "probably one-third were sacrificed at auction."[1] Nothing daunted by this, but encouraged by the favorable opinion expressed by "some of the most experienced and intelligent men in our country," Raymond in 1823 gave to the unappreciative public a second, and revised edition of his work:[2]

The principles laid down in the first edition were not departed from, nor modified. The asperity that marked its tone was somewhat softened, and much harsh criticism of Adam Smith was omitted—though sufficient of this latter crops out in the second edition to satisfy a moderate opponent of "foreign systems." The arrangement of the work

---

[1] *Ibid.*, p. 9.

[2] In the second edition Raymond omits the unique preface that introduced the first, and in its place writes: "On presenting the public with a second edition of this work, the author feels himself constrained to express his gratitude for the kind reception, which the first hasty and imperfect edition met with, from a portion of his fellow-citizens. It was not to be expected, that a work, whatever might be its merits, upon so abstruse and forbidding a subject as political economy, would command the attention of the generality of readers in any country; and it would indeed be a wonder, if a book on any subject, written on the wrong side of the Atlantic, with the author's name to it, should be favorably received by the public generally. Our independence is not sufficiently established for that.

"But as some of the most experienced and intelligent men in our country have expressed a favorable opinion of the model, (for the first edition was but a model), and intimated that it was susceptible of being executed in such a manner as to be worthy of public patronage, the author felt himself not only justified, but required to make another effort to improve the work."

was altered, several chapters were recast, and a few new ones added, developing special topics that were of secondary importance in Raymond's system.

A copy of this second edition found its way to England, and was pronounced by "Blackwood's" "a work of extraordinary value;" but this criticism was that of an American temporarily resident in London,—a personal acquaintance, likely, and possibly even a friend of Raymond—and does not represent an English estimate of the value of the work. It was unable to secure a review at the hands of an English reviewer.[1]

The second edition appears to have met with as little popular favor as the first. Its sale was "very slow and limited," and Raymond seems to have been "a considerable loser" as the result of trying to furnish his fellow-citizens with a system of political economy of domestic manufacture. The ⁻

---

[1] In 1820 a series of articles appeared in "Blackwood's" on "American Writers." They purported to be from the pen of an Englishman, but the real author was John Neal, "a Yankee, from Maine," and, like Raymond, at one time a member of the Baltimore bar. Neal gave up the practice of law for literature, and spent the years 1823-27 in England, where he was a frequent contributor to the British periodicals. His reference to Raymond is in his series on "American Writers," in Blackwood's for February, 1825, Vol. XVII., p. 200, and is as follows: "Daniel Raymond; a Yankee; from Connecticut, New England; a counsellor at law; author of a work on political economy, (2 vols. 8vo.), where a multitude of problems, phenomena, etc., etc., are explained with a simplicity quite startling—nay, quite provoking—to those who have been wasting years upon the science. We look upon it as a work of extraordinary value. It should have been republished here; or, at least, reviewed. A friend of ours (Neal) brought a copy "out," and exerted himself not a little, in trying to get some notice taken of it, by somebody equal to the job. Twice he was promised, without qualification, that it should be done. Twice he was disappointed. He then gave up the point." While in London Neal lived for considerable time with Jeremy Bentham, and was intimate with the little group of utilitarians, and economists, who used to meet periodically in Bentham's study. Was it possibly to one of these that he gave Raymond's treatise for review?

two editions together numbered only twelve hundred and
fifty copies, and whilst each had failed of complete sale,
Say's treatise had, during the same time, been translated and
republished here in two editions,—the first of seven hundred
and fifty, and the second of two thousand copies—and both
had been sold out. Some two thousand copies of reprints of
Adam Smith had also been taken up by the American public.[1] These facts scarcely bear out Raymond's complaint
that "a very small portion of the intelligent reading part of
the community ever think of reading a book upon the subject" of political economy, and indicate that the indifference
which Jefferson lamented in 1815 was passing away.

The failure of Raymond's work to win popular favor is not
in itself sufficient to convict the public of his day of an indifference to his science; the cause of this failure may more
properly be sought in the character of the work itself. It
was not without merit; in many respects it was worthy of the
attention of the time, and merited a more careful and con-
siderate perusal than it received. But looseness of method
marked it, and frequently confusion of ideas; and in addition
it touched upon too many questions that were then the cen-
ters of political storms. On one side or another it found
itself in opposition to some popular prejudice. It ran counter to the philosophy of individualism, which was the accepted gospel of the elect of those days. Its advocacy of
protection was too liberal to please the more rabid advocates
of an "American System," and too pronounced, on the other
hand, to win readers from amongst the strict disciples of
laissez faire. Its intolerant opposition to banks and to all
forms of corporations destroyed the value of his work in the
eyes of the advocates of these institutions. His fierce hatred
of slavery was a fatal obstacle to popularity in the South.
It is more than probable that the unstinted praise and admiration the work elicited from John Adams was not due
so much to any real merit it possessed as a scientific treatise
as from the fact that Adams was a Federalist and believed
in strong central government, stood for protection, abhorred

---

[1]Carey, Biographical Sketches, p. 9.

banks and paper money,[1] and loathed slavery;[2] and that in all these things he found in Raymond a kindred spirit. But Adams' type was not numerous. The men who agreed with Raymond in the matter of the province of government and of protection, would not have subscribed to his views on the banks; and those who would have been in agreement with his views on banks, were repelled by his position on slavery.

Raymond's second edition scarcely attracted the attention of even the reviewers, and little notice of it appears until 1825. A report then started the rounds of the press,—originating apparently with his friend and defender, the *Federal Gazette*, of Baltimore—to the effect that the work had been adopted in the University of Virginia as the standard textbook on political economy;[3] but this was promptly, and emphatically, denied by the Richmond *Enquirer*.[4]

---

[1]"I have never had but one opinion concerning banking, from the institution of the first in Philadelphia, by Mr. Robert Morris, and Mr. Gouverneur Morris, and that opinion has uniformly been that the banks have done more injury to the religion, morality, tranquility, prosperity, and even wealth of the nation, than they can have done or ever will do good. They are like party spirit, the delusion of the many for the benefit of the few." "Works," Vol. X., p. 375.

"Our whole banking system I ever abhorred, I continue to abhor, and I shall die abhorring. . . . . Every bank of discount, every bank by which interest is to be paid, or profit of any kind made by the deponent, is downright corruption. . . . . Every bank in the Union ought to be annihilated, and every bank of discount prohibited to all eternity." *Ibid.*, Vol. IX., p. 638.

[2]*Ibid.*, Vol. X., p. 381.

[3]"We feel gratified to learn that the work of our fellow-citizen, Mr. Raymond, on political economy, has been adopted in the University of Virginia, as the standard work on that subject in that institution. When we consider the high political as well as literary reputation of the gentlemen who are at the head of that institution, among whom are the two ex-Presidents, Jefferson and Madison, we cannot but think this a most flattering compliment to the work, and one which can not fail to establish its reputation with the American people." *Federal Gazette*, June, 1825.

[4]"A paragraph from a Baltimore paper is now going the rounds,

In 1836 Raymond seems to have believed the time ripe for the acceptance of his principles, and he accordingly issued a third edition of his work. It was identical with the edition of thirteen years before, except for the addition of a chapter on "Tariffs," discussing the incidence of an impost tax. Other than this, not a word nor a comma was changed from the second edition. The two editions appear to have been struck from the same plates.

Of the fate of this edition I can find no traces. It must have met with more success than the preceding ones, for in 1840 Raymond was encouraged to put out a fourth edition. The second and third editions had been issued in two volumes, in large type, thus forming a bulky and unhandy treatise. Believing, probably, that a more compact and handy volume would be more acceptable to the public, he compressed the work in the fourth edition into one small volume. In essentials—with one exception to be noted—it was practically the same work that had appeared twenty years before, and twice at subsequent periods. The last edition could not so much be called revised, as condensed. The process of condensation consisted in omitting entirely several of the chapters added in the second edition, and others that had appeared in the original edition, and in shortening the remaining chapters by the wholesale cutting out of paragraph after paragraph, and even of page after page. It must be admitted that the constant repetitions that characterized the book made it peculiarly suited to this sort of revision.

We are left to surmise to account for the appearance, in comparatively rapid succession, of these last two editions,

---

viz., that 'the work of Mr. Raymond on Political Economy, has been adopted in the University of Virginia as the standard work on that subject.' Having some reasons to doubt the correctness of such an assertion, while such works as Say, Ricardo, Adam Smith, &c., are in existence, we requested a friend to ascertain the facts; and we are now enabled to state positively that Mr. Raymond's work is not used as the text-book at the university, and that it is not known there except to Mr. Tucker, and possibly to Mr. Emmett." *Rich. Enq.*, July 1, 1825.

after the little success that had attended the earlier ones. During the thirteen years elapsing between the second and third editions Raymond had apparently given little thought to economics. Had he done so, and kept abreast of the development of the science, he would hardly have made his third edition a mere reprint of his second. The public seem to have grown to value him more as a lawyer than as an economist, and to have given him sufficient employment in his chief profession to prevent the necessity of his again having to seek diversion in formulating new economic theories. In his fourth edition he devotes some thirty pages to a commentary on the constitution. Such a discussion was perfectly germane to his subject, as he conceived it. The idea of writing it, was suggested to him by Provost Beasley in his letter of 1824, but in the preface to his fourth edition, Raymond explains that he had "had no leisure until lately, to write such a treatise." The intervening sixteen years, we may infer, had been a busy period for him in his regular profession, and had left no time for authorship.

In 1836 economic issues were more than ever the bone of political contention; and it is likely that the triumph of Jackson and the hard money party over the bank, the increase of the abolition sentiment, and the struggle that was going on to bring about a return to protective principles, led Raymond to think the time opportune for the acceptance of his doctrines. This assumption is supported by the fact that the only change in the edition of 1836 is the addition of a chapter on tariffs; and that in the edition of 1840, whilst many chapters are omitted, and most of the remaining ones pruned severely, the chapter on slavery is left untouched; the one on banking is modified only by the addition of a paragraph arguing against the constitutionality of the bank; the one on money is likewise left untouched save for the addition of a paragraph; the chapter on tariffs, added in the third edition, is retained; and the chapter on corporations is entirely rewritten,—and from rabid opposition changes to mild tolerance of these organizations. The preface also adduces the political history of the preceding twenty years as an exemplification of the truth of Raymond's principles.

This fourth edition seems to have impressed John Quincy Adams as much as the first one had impressed his distinguished father. The son was at that time waging the battle of abolition in the national house of representatives with all his strength, and it is quite possible that it was Raymond's vehement chapter on slavery that won the admiration of this valiant champion, rather than the general soundness of his economic principles. At all events, he deemed the work worthy of the perusal of his fellow-statesman, and he found time, between presentations of abolition petitions, to make a formal presentation of a copy of Raymond's book to the library of the house of representatives. But there were those among his colleagues who could not find it in their hearts to share the admiration of Mr. Adams for the book, and the question of its acceptance created a scene in the national house that is worthy of note as indicating the standards by which a scientific treatise on economics was judged a half century ago, and the storm of prejudice it had to weather.[1]

---

[1] House of Representatives; June 23, 1840:

"Mr. Adams presented a work on political economy, by Daniel Raymond, of Maryland; which, on motion of Mr. A. was ordered to be placed in the library of the House of Representatives."
June 24, 1840.

"Mr. Jones moved to go into committee of the whole on the state of the union, but temporarily withdrew his motion at the request of Mr. Crabb, of Alabama, who moved a reconsideration of the decision made yesterday to receive and place in the library of the House of Representatives, a copy of Raymond's Political Economy. Having examined that book, Mr. Crabb had discovered that it contained doctrine and language highly exceptionable to him as a Southern man; in case of reconsideration, he wished to move the reference of the book to the committee on the library, in order that it might be examined and reported on.

II.

In all its principles Raymond's system stands opposed to the orthodox political economy of his time.   He alleges against the prevailing school, that it has failed to grasp the true concept of national wealth, and has therefore missed the real aim of true *political* economy; that it has studied how individuals may increase their wealth, assuming that national wealth was nothing other than the sum total of individual wealth, and that consequently the study of how individual

---

Mr. Turney demanded the previous question on the motion to reconsider.   The previous question was seconded, put and carried; and the main question being on reconsidering, Mr. Jones demanded the yeas and nays, which were ordered.   Mr. Adams rose amidst cries of order, and was going on to express his surprise at the motion of the gentleman from Alabama, and to give some account of the book, when he was arrested by the chair.   Mr. A. remonstrated.   The chair insisted that he could not proceed, but by general consent.   Objections were loudly uttered.

Mr. Lincoln said that unless his colleague were permitted to proceed and give the House some account of the book, Mr. L. should demand that the book itself be read.   Objections being made, Mr. Lincoln demanded that the book be read.   The chair decided that as the gentleman from Massachusetts (Mr. Lincoln) was called to vote respecting this book, he had a right, under the rules of the House, to have it read, if he so demanded.   Great confusion arose. Messrs. Habersham, Turney, Andrews, Hopkins, and others were on their feet, all simultaneously addressing the chair.   Mr. Hopkins called for the reading of the rule of the house, and also of Mr. Jefferson's manual on the question of order.   Mr. Lincoln wished to explain, but the chair refused, the previous question having been ordered.   The chair then stated his decision, and explained the ground on which it rested.

Mr. Hopkins took an appeal; before any vote was taken on the appeal, Mr. Ramsay moved to lay the whole subject on the table. Mr. Crabb wished to explain, but was arrested.   The question being stated from the chair, Mr. Adams addressed the House. (Loud

wealth is augmented is at the same time the study of how
national wealth is augmented; that it has, therefore, busied
itself with the study of value, a phenomenon with which
political economy has little concern.[1] In opposition to this,
he contends that national wealth is something far other than
the sum total of individual wealth; that the two are not even
composed of the same ingredients; and that an increase in
the wealth of one class of citizens does not of necessity imply
an equal increase in national wealth.

Distinguishing national from individual wealth, Raymond
defines the former as "a capacity for acquiring the necessaries and comforts of life," by labor.[2] Capacity, not com-

---

cries of order.) The gentleman from Alaba— the chair called to
order. The gentleman from Alabama has undertaken (order! order!) to be grand inquisitor for this House; to speak (order!) its
opinion on a certain book. (Here the cries of order were very
loud, and the chair ordered Mr. Adams to resume his seat.) The
question being again stated Mr. Crabb demanded the yeas and nays,
but the house refused to order them. The vote being taken, the
chair, declared it to be decided in the affirmative.

The question was again put, and the House dividing, the yeas
were 123 and the noes 30. So the House determined that the whole
subject should be laid on the table.

[1]"According to the theory suggested in the preceding chapter, it
will follow that *value* has very little application to public wealth; a
very small ingredient or portion only of national wealth being the
subject of value." p. 84, (4th ed.)

Unless otherwise specified, succeeding references are to Raymond's 4th ed.

[2]"This capacity never can exist independent of labor. Its extent, however, will depend upon a great variety of other circumstances. It will be materially influenced by the nature of the government. The energies of a nation, can be more fully developed
under a free, than under an arbitrary or tyranical government.

"This capacity will also depend materially upon the climate and
soil of a country; on the extent of territory in proportion to the
number of inhabitants; on the denseness of the population; upon
the equal or unequal division of property; upon the state of cultivation and improvements; on the degree of perfection to which the
arts and sciences have been carried; on the nation's advantageous
situation for commerce, and especially on the industrious econom-
ical habits of the people." p. 81.

modities, constitutes national wealth.

This concept of national wealth is the first characteristic principle of Raymond's system. The second is his insistence upon the recognition of the idea of a nation as an organic unit. The existing systems of political economy do not, he maintains, so conceive the nation. They have, in turn, mistaken the interests of one or another class for the interests of the nation as a whole; whereas the interest of an individual or a class may be opposed to the larger interest of the nation as one and indivisible.

From these two principles, Raymond argues that it is not the province of political economy to study how values are created and augmented, and how individuals or classes may acquire wealth; but rather to study how government may best legislate to secure the greatest well-being to all citizens alike.[1] Such questions, therefore, as value, rent, wages, profit, and interest, Raymond discusses only in passing;[2] they belong properly to individual economy, and not to national economy. The topics that concern him as a political economist, are the larger questions that operate directly and strongly on national wealth, and with which legislative policy must therefore concern itself.

Labor is the sole cause of wealth;[3] labor power is wealth,— and accordingly Raymond devotes a chapter to labor. He objects to Adam Smith's classification of labor as productive and unproductive. All labor is productive, except such as fails of its intended effect.[4] Instead therefore of this classification, he distinguishes labor as *productive* and as *permanent*. The end of productive labor is to produce things for direct consumption; of permanent labor, "to enlarge the boundaries of knowledge, and to augment the capacity for acquiring the necessaries and comforts of life."[5]

---

[1]P. 116.

[2]Rent, wages, profit, and interest, were not discussed in the first edition of the work. Short chapters were devoted to them in the second edition, but were omitted again from the fourth.

[3]"Labour is the cause, and the only cause of wealth." p. 97.

[4]P. 90.   [5]P. 95.

A chapter is devoted to "Production and Consumption." In it Raymond attacks the "absurd doctrine of augmenting national wealth by accumulation;" maintaining that any excess of production above consumption produces stagnation and distress rather than wealth and prosperity. National prosperity is promoted only when all the fruits of productive labor are annually consumed; and national wealth is augmented when wise political institutions so operate as to direct a due proportion of the energies of the nation towards permanent labor.

Raymond next discusses Agriculture, Manufacture, and Commerce, in their influence upon national wealth. "Each of these three great departments of labor, has had its partisans, who have claimed for it the superiority over the others, as most conducive to national wealth. It is, however, manifest that in a national point of view they are but parts of one great system, each of them essential to the other."[1] The proportion that ought to exist between them will depend on circumstances and vary in different nations, and the wise legislator will encourage or restrain them in such way as will, in the circumstances of that nation, best advance national wealth and prosperity.

On the subject of money Raymond stands with the "hard money" school. He insists on "the necessity of intrinsic value in whatever is used as money; and the utter impossibility of giving a nominal value to money, above its intrinsic value as a commodity or as bullion."[2] He holds unquestioningly to the quantity theory, and to the currency principle. He insists that to the government alone belongs the function of furnishing money, whether coin or "representative paper," and that this function should never be entrusted to individuals or corporate bodies. The "manufacture" of credit money is merely "an ingenuous contrivance upon the public" for the benefit of the banks, and is at variance with

---

[1]P. 117.   [2]P. 165.

sound monetary principles. If a paper currency be needed, it should be issued by the government, and "whenever a paper dollar is put in circulation, a silver dollar should be withdrawn from circulation."[1]

To "the credit system, which has ruined so many people,"[2] Raymond is in general opposed; and towards the banks, promoters of this destructive system, he is thoroughly hostile. As "depositories of money and other valuable articles," and as offices for buying and selling bills of exchange and discounting real notes, banks are solely beneficial to the public; but by uniting in themselves the double function of loan office and of "manufacturers of paper money" they are a constant menace to prosperity, and invariably cause many and grave public evils. "By being loan offices, they are enabled to loan all the money they can make, or at least, as much as they please; and by being the manufacturers of a paper currency, they are enabled to make as much money as they can loan. So long as these two functions are united in the same body, they must and will be exercised to the prejudice of the public."[3]   Nothing but the "good sense of the community has prevented the principle upon which the banks are established, from being carried to such an extreme as to ruin the country;"—had it been otherwise, and nothing interfered to prevent them from following out the dictates of their interests, the banks would "have become possessed of every foot of property in the country, which would have been paid to them in the shape of interest for their money."[4] Against banks Raymond lays specific indictments:

"They increase the quantity of circulating medium, and thereby depreciate its value."[5]

"Banks enable money lenders to obtain usurious interest for their actual money."[6]

"Banks promote extravagant speculation."[7]

---

[1]P. 175. [2]P. 153. [3]P. 178. [4]*Ibid.* [5]P. 180. [6]P. 186. [7]P. 188.

"Banks cause sudden fluctuations in the value of property, and consequently produce extensive failures."[1]

"Banks have a tendency to banish the precious metals from the country."[2]

To remedy "the evils of the banking or credit system," Raymond proposes three alternative plans.[3] These evils, as has been pointed out, result from uniting in one body the two functions of loan office and manufacturer of paper currency. Therefore, let the power of issue be taken from the banks entirely, and reserved to the government; or, let their issues be regulated in amount by the government; or, if they must be allowed "to retain the power of manufacturing their own notes to as great an extent as they please," let there be taken from them "the motive to loan more than a certain amount of their paper in proportion to the amount of their capital."

The first plan proposes the issue by government of paper money, on the strict currency principle, as outlined in his discussion of money.[4] If this method be adopted, all evils in any way connected with the banking system can be cured, by the simple, but drastic process of abolishing the whole banking system,—"which may be done without any inconvenience to the public."[5]

The second plan proposes that the banks be limited in the issue of their notes to a certain ratio of their paid-up capital, —all notes to be engraved by the government and delivered to the banks for signature and issuance only upon proof of the actual amount of paid-up capital. This plan is, in effect, almost identical with the one adopted by Congress in 1863 as the basis of the national bank issues.[6] The third plan proposes that, in case this second one should be thought impracticable, a maximum rate be fixed by law for bank divi-

---

[1]*Ibid.* [2]P. 189. [3]Pp. 192-3. [4]Supra; pp. 31-2. [5]P. 193.

[6]Raymond's plan, in view of its close resemblance to the plan adopted for controlling the national bank issues, is worth quoting in

dends, and all surplus profits over and above this rate be appropriated by the government for the public benefit.

Raymond also argues against the constitutionality of a national bank, on the ground that it is virtually turning over to a corporation the prerogative of acting as a regulator of the circulating medium; and that as this function partakes of the nature of a legislative rather than a ministerial act, it cannot be delegated by congress.[1]

To the subject of "Finance," Raymond devotes little space. That branch of the science of political economy is important indeed, but has been exalted into undue pre-eminence. A stateman's abilities are usually estimated by his adroitness and skill in "diverting a portion of the stream of public wealth into the public treasury," whereas "true political skill consists in an ability to augment the stream itself of public wealth."[2] As to the general injurious effect of taxation upon production, Raymond takes issue with Smith, Say, and Ricardo, and maintains that taxes judiciously expended may so act as to augment *national* wealth, rather than

---

detail. "If we must have a bank paper currency, it seems proper that it should be under the control of the. government. If the government will not adopt the plan suggested in the chapter on money, let it take into its own hands the engraving and manufacturing of bank notes, all except the signatures, and establish a mint, and appoint officers under proper responsibility, for that purpose. The banks are to be permitted to issue no paper except what they obtain at this office of the government. The government is then to determine the amount of paper the banks are to be permitted to loan in proportion to the amount of their capital—and upon the incorporation of a bank, and proof being furnished of the amount of specie or capital paid in, so much paper is to be furnished the bank as the government has fixed upon, as the quantity the bank may issue in proportion to the amount of its capital. In some such way as this, it would seem that the banks might be restrained from excessive issues of a paper currency." p. 193.

This chapter was written in 1820.

[1] P. 194. [2] P. 237.

affect it injuriously—however they may affect individuals or classes.[1] Equality of taxation is to be sought with reference to persons, not to property. Indirect are to be preferred to direct taxes. Taxes are classified, land tax, excise tax, and imposts. Of these imposts have an undoubted preference over either of the other forms. As between a land tax and an excise tax advantages are divided.[2]

Rabid hostility towards all "money corporations" characterizes Raymond at the beginning of his career as an economist. So far as is possible in civil society, the "natural equality" of men should be preserved. To this end government should bend its efforts. Money corporations are "artificial engines of power, contrived by the rich, for the purpose of increasing their already too great ascendency, and calculated to destroy that natural equality among men, which no government ought to lend its power in destroying." "Corporations are, therefore, *prima facie*, injurious to national wealth."[3] But in his last edition (1840) Raymond grows more discriminating in his condemnations. He suggests merely legislative supervision over the most objectionable forms of *public* corporations, for, "then they become the mere agents of the legislature to accomplish a public good." As

---

[1] Pp. 247-8.

[2] "Imposts have an undoubted preference over all other taxes. are indirect, and are, therefore, paid voluntarily. They are levied and collected when the goods are in the hands of the fewest persons, and are, therefore, collected with the least expense and they have the very important advantage of securing to domestic industry a preference in the home market. In other words, they are equal as affects citizens, and unequal as between citizens and foreigners, to the amount of the difference between the imposts and an excise tax upon the same kind of produce. If the tax was equal upon domestic and foreign products, then foreigners would stand upon an equality with citizens in the home market, while citizens probably would not stand upon an equality with foreigners in their own market." p. 255.

[3] P. 121, Vol. I., 2nd ed.

for private corporations, "they may be multiplied indefinitely, without detriment to the public, provided they are secured against the depredations of stock jobbers."[1]   In 1836, he writes, "the very object then of the act of incorporation is to produce inequality, either in rights or in the division of property."[2]   In 1840, "the only effect of the charter of incorporation is to make unity out of a multitude, so as to enable them to act as an individual in one name, and to transfer and transmit their property, without the legal impediments and hindrances which attend partnership transactions."[3]   The point of view that marks the editions of 1820, 1823, and 1836, is very far from the one that characterizes the edition of 1840; the philosophy of a lifetime suffers violent metamorphosis within four years.

As would be expected from the basis of his system, Raymond favors a protective system.   He does not, as would have been most logical, and as List did later, develop his protective doctrine directly from his two fundamental concepts.   He was too much haunted by the spectre of Adam Smith, and too much possessed by the idea of refuting his system point by point.   Instead, therefore, of attempting to build up a logical and consistent system, which in its conclusions should stand opposed to those of the school of Smith, he is constantly shifting his position and adapting his arguments to the purpose of refuting Smith specifically point by point.   He denies the assumption that each individual in seeking his own interest will employ his capital in the way most beneficial to the nation, and he therefore justifies governmental restriction on the ground of its tending to promote the welfare of the nation as a whole.

He admits as a general rule that if a nation can buy an article cheaper than it can make it, it is better to buy than to make; but the numerous exceptions to this rule "will em-

---

[1]P. 275.   [2]P. 119, 2nd ed.   [3]P. 275.

brace the policy of protecting duties to as great an extent, as has ever been contended for by the partisans of a restricted trade."[1]   A protective system is required in the interest of the nation as a whole in order to give constant employment to its whole labor force.[2]   Further, though the initial cost of producing certain articles should be more than would be required to purchase them abroad, their average cost of production in the long run ought to be taken into account rather than initial cost.[3]

A monopoly of the home market produces certainty and stability of demand;[4] it increases a nation's skill in the arts and sciences, and thus increases its capacity for acquiring the necessaries and comforts of life,—increases national wealth.[5]   Unless the people of this country are to be "reduced to the necessity of working as hard and living as poor, as the English laborers," a tariff must be maintained to enable our manufacturers to compete with those of England in a great variety of articles.[6]   But even could we produce as cheaply as England, a tariff would still be required to prevent the *surplus* product of British manufacture from being irregularly dumped on our market and demoralizing prices, to the destruction of our home manufactories.[7]

A tariff requires constant revision. The general rule is stated that "a tariff ought not to be reduced, although it may frequently require to be raised;" "and it should be lowest upon those articles which are not, or cannot be produced in this country, and highest upon those which employ the greatest number of people, or the greatest portion of the industry of the country."[8]   Under the head of tariffs, Raymond discusses the question of who pays the duty. By a strictly "*a priori*" process of reasoning he reaches the con-

---

[1]P. 216. [2]P. 218. [3]P. 223. [4]P. 224. [5]P. 224. [6]P. 225. [7]P. 226.
[8]P. 226.

clusion that the producer and consumer share between them the burden of the tax.[1]

In conclusion he hurls maledictions at slavery, as a moral blight and an economic curse. It acts as a check on population, and thus exerts a pernicious influence on national wealth and prosperity. Legislation must devise the most effective means to root out this obstacle to national prosperity.

---

[1] P. 231.

CHAPTER III.

Genesis of Raymond's System.

I.

A brief outline of Raymond's system has been given. How are we to trace its genesis? The tendency of much of the economic thought in this country in Raymond's time was plainly begotten of hostility towards England and all that was English; but in Raymond's case there is no justification whatever for the statement that we can trace his inspiration to this source.[1] On the contrary, there is every reason to believe that his economic views were the natural consequence of a study of the phenomena that confronted him on every side. He did not adopt his principles to be in opposition to Adam Smith; he was in opposition to Adam Smith because his principles landed him there. He was confronted—and deeply impressed—by a slave power grown to threatening proportions, and bidding fair to turn backward the current of national prosperity; he had seen trade wrecked and industry paralyzed by reckless banking, and the business community powerless to protect itself; he had seen great manufacturing interests grow up around him—a source of

---

[1] Furber—p. 58, of his Geschichte und kritische Studien zur Entwickelung der Oekonomischen Theorien in Amerika—says that Raymond was not free from the hatred of England so prevalent at that time in this country; and Cossa, p. 465, says, "Daniel Raymond, the first of all the spokesmen for American national and protective theories, was partly inspired to his utterance of them by animosity against England." A careful reading of Raymond's work scarcely bears out Furber's statement; and as for Cossa, he could hardly have read Raymond at all, as there is, in fact, not a line in any of his four editions that would even suggest animosity against England as the motive impelling him to write his work. On the contrary, considering the time, the subject, and our relations towards England, there is a most marked absence in Raymond of anything savoring of animosity towards England.

power and wealth to the nation—only to be threatened with annihilation by the pent-up flood of British wares that deluged the country after the return of peace in 1815; and he, in consequence, began to entertain doubts as to the wisdom and practicability of a system of political economy that ignored the existence of national boundaries, assumed for its philosophy "the harmony of interests," and preached for its gospel *laissez faire.* He thought that he saw a necessity for governmental restriction to check the selfish and short-sighted policy of individuals, and to keep the nation as a whole in the path of prosperity. He is accordingly led to the belief that the prevailing systems of political economy are not adapted to the circumstances of this country;[1] and he sets out to study our peculiar conditions, and to develop a system of political economy that will harmonize with the observed facts of our economic life, and serve to light the way for legislation beneficial to American interests.

Around him he saw a young country with undeveloped resources that dazzled the imagination, and in which it was emphatically true that power was wealth. Its wealth and prosperity could not be gauged by the same standards as would individual wealth and prosperity. An individual who steadily buys more than he sells is supposed to be on the road to poverty; but here was a nation, here were commonwealths, that for decades had bought more than they sold, and which were yet recognized as increasing in real wealth out of all proportion to their accumulating debts.[2] Even in popular parlance, not the *stock* of the country, but its productive capacity was regarded as the evidence of its wealth and progress. Raymond came thus naturally to his characteristic concept of national wealth.

His sympathy rests with what we term the masses. These he believes to have been ignored in former treatises professing to be concerned with the *nation's* wealth;[3] and in his system he desires to take account of them and their interests.

---

[1] P. 5, 1st ed.   [2] P. 129.   [3] P. 43, 2nd ed.

He was a lawyer, and his legal habit of mind leads him to conceive the state as a corporation,[1] and gives him a formula that fits his need.   Thus he comes to his second basic concept of a nation as an organic unity, composed of all its citizens alike, "a unity of rights, interests and possessions."

A study of Raymond's work, then, suggests environment and training as the sources of his fundamental concepts, rather than hostility towards England.

As for the rest, he is lacking in method.   He is partly deductive, partly inductive;   but neither consistent nor discriminating in the use of either method.   He studies conditions as they confront him, but his inferences are often colored to a degree by his prepossessions.   He rejects Adam Smith's principle that the individual in seeking out his own best interests necessarily advances the interests of society, because it will not square with the facts standing out in bold relief in American economic life.   But despite the benefits that a community may derive from "money corporations," he condemns them indiscriminately because they are opposed in principle to his social philosophy that the natural equality of man is to be preserved as far as possible in civil society.   He argues against the doctrine of augmenting national wealth by accumulation, because he conceives the law of nature to be that production should only keep pace with consumption; nature antagonizes the storing up of her fruits; and the story of the Hebrews and the manna in the desert is for him a conclusive exemplification of the operation of this law.[2]   "In the sweat of thy face shalt thou eat bread,"[3] he erects into a scientific formula, and makes it serve as a basis for deductions.   He even inclines to allow his strong human feeling and his sense of Providence to supply the place of analysis and logic.[4]

The strong sense of personality, the warm human sympathy, the realization that man, not matter, is the subject of his

---

[1] P. 272.   [2] P. 103.   [3] P. 70.

[4] "Mr. Malthus' theory of population is certainly ingenuous and plausible, and for the most part sound, although it is calculated to

study, that wealth is a means, not an end, that his science is human, not mechanical,—these things stand out in Raymond in contradistinction to the cold formalism, the chilling abstractness of the classic economics of that day,—and almost make one forgiving toward serious lapses from scientific method.

II.

Raymond seems to have been familiar with Adam Smith, Malthus, Ricardo, Lauderdale, Ganilh and J. B. Say.[1] The system of the Physiocrats he knew only partially, and at second hand.[2]

He is in opposition to the system of Adam Smith at nearly every point, and his criticism of ‹Smith—especially in his first edition—is narrow and harsh.   Say he rates as inferior

leave very erroneous impressions on the mind of the reader, in consequence of his not having treated the subject in conjunction with others with which it is necessarily connected. Although his theory is founded upon the principles of nature, and although it is impossible to discover any flaw in his reasoning, yet the mind instinctively revolts at the conclusions to which he conducts it, and we are disposed to reject the theory, even though we could give no good reason for rejecting it." p. 273, 1st ed.

[1] Raymond had not read Say when he published his first edition in 1820, for Say had not then been translated in this country, and Raymond in his second edition—(V. I., p. 174),—says he has read Say only in the translation. But reading Say does not appear to have modified any of Raymond's views.

[2] Raymond, in several places, refers directly to the Physiocrats in a way that would suggest an acquaintance with them, and this impression is confirmed by the reference in his second edition—(V. I., p. 97)—of a quotation direct to "Physiocratie, p. 107." The quotation, however, is taken at second hand, from Lauderdale, p. 125, and not directly from "Physiocratie," as would seem. In his first edi-

to both Adam Smith and Malthus.[1] Of Malthus he appears
to have a favorable estimate, and several times quotes him
approvingly.[2] Of Ricardo he expresses no opinion; he refers to him in the chapter on taxation, only to refute him.

Lauderdale is undoubtedly the author who exerted the
most influence upon Raymond. The general plan of Raymond's treatise is somewhat similar to that of Lauderdale,—
first, an inquiry into the concept of wealth, its cause, and its
source, and then a discussion of the means by which national wealth may be promoted.[3]

Raymond follows Lauderdale in distinguishing individual
from national wealth, and, like him, makes this the basic
principle upon which he erects his system. He says that
Lauderdale is the only writer known to him who makes this
distinction;[4] and it is most probable that it was this distinction of Lauderdale that first led Raymond to seek in a new
concept of national wealth the basis for what seemed to him
the true system of political economy.[5] But Raymond does
not appropriate Lauderdale's idea bodily; he gets from it no
more than a suggestion as to the lines along which study
may profitably be made.[6]

---

tion, p. 92, he says in a foot note that he has never read any of the
writings of the Physiocrats, his only knowledge of their theories being "derived from Smith, Ganilh, and others, who have combatted
their theories."

[1]" . . . in comprehensiveness of views, and in the powers of
reasoning, M. Say is vastly inferior, both to Adam Smith and Malthus." P. 173, 2nd ed.

[2]Pp. 129, 169; V. I., p. 354; V. II., 2nd ed.

[3]Comp. Raymond, pp. 3-4, Vol. II., 2nd ed., and Lauderdale, introduction.

[4]"Lord Lauderdale is, I believe, the only writer on political economy, who has attempted to distinguish national from individual
wealth." P. 174, 2nd ed.

[5]"His lordship, however, deserves great credit for having suggested the fundamental principles of the science, although he failed
in stating it with precision."

[6]"But although the noble earl was impressed with an idea of the
existence of such a distinction in the nature of things, and the neces-

The distinction which Raymond makes between national and individual wealth is his own, not Lauderdale's. The basis on which the distinction rests is very different in the two writers. Lauderdale makes no specific difference between the *things* that go to constitute individual riches and those that go to constitute public wealth. He makes public wealth "to consist of all that man desires as useful or delightful to him;" and private riches "to consist of all that man desires as useful or delightful to him; which exists in a degree of scarcity."[1] Thus, the objects that enter into the two categories are only differentiated by the accidental attribute, scarcity; there is no essential difference in the things themselves. Any object that is embraced under either category, is capable of being embraced under the other. Public wealth is in reality only a slightly more generic concept than individual riches, and anything included under it can be included also under the less extensive concept, individual riches, by simply coming to exist in a degree of scarcity.

Raymond, on the contrary, founds the main difference between the concepts of individual wealth and national wealth upon a radical and essential difference in the nature of the things that are embraced under the two concepts. To him individual wealth means "the possession of property, for the use of which, the owner can obtain a quantity of the necessaries and comforts of life."[2] The term property "includes lands, goods, money, and stock," and "the value of these that an individual possesses, ascertains the amount of his

---

sity of pointing it out, and establishing it as the basis of the science, yet he has utterly failed in his attempts to ascertain in what this distinction consists. P. 175, 2nd ed.

"Although Lord Lauderdale had conceived some indistinct notion of the difference between national and individual wealth, yet as he did not preserve the unity of the nation, and a consequent unity of its interests, he did not succeed in establishing the distinction he had imperfectly conceived."

[1] "An Inquiry into the Nature and Causes of Public Wealth." Pp. 56-7.

[2] P. 77.

wealth." Individual wealth is thus made to consist of *commodities;* value is its measure; and exchange-ability its distinguishing characteristic.

National wealth is something quite different from this. It is defined, a capacity for acquiring, by labor, the necessaries and comforts of life. It is thus made to consist, not of objective goods, but of forces, of labor power. The two concepts are generically different. The things embraced under the concept of national wealth could not possibly be made to come under the category of individual wealth.

With Lauderdale, water, for example, is public wealth, and it may also be made to come under the term private wealth, if it become so diminished in quantity as to exist in a degree of scarcity. But with Raymond, the labor power, the energy, and the habits of the community constitute elements in its national wealth; and these can not be brought under his concept of private wealth.

While Raymond and Lauderdale are thus similar in that they both distinguish public from private wealth, there is no similarity in the distinctions themselves which they make. Raymond's concept of national wealth bears no trace of similarity to that of Lauderdale. There is nothing in Lauderdale to furnish even a suggestion of such a definition of national wealth as Raymond gives; and his system thus appears to be based upon an original, and not upon a borrowed idea.

So too in attacking the thesis of Adam Smith, that "parsimony and not industry is the immediate cause of the increase of capital," Raymond is found sustaining the same theory as Lauderdale; but again his arguments are other than Lauderdale's, and seem to have been in no way derived from him.

It may be again repeated, that in these cases the influence of American conditions and of the phenomena here confronting Raymond appear as more potent factors in determining his conclusions than do the theories or arguments of Lauderdale.

CHAPTER IV.

DANIEL RAYMOND AND FRIEDERICH LIST.

There is a striking similarity at bottom between Raymond's theories and "The National System of Political Economy" developed by Friederich List.

It is not too much to say that not only is the germ of List's system to be found in Raymond, but that a very considerable development is to be found scattered through his eight hundred and odd pages.[1] The theory is not developed by Raymond with anything like the elaboration and continuity that characterize List's treatment of it. But it will be recalled that Raymond was only a political economist incidentally; a lawyer to whom the public permitted too many moments of leisure to be whiled away in the conning of musty tomes; who sought diversion in putting on paper some of his thoughts on economics; and who wrote, accordingly, rather for his own amusement than for the public. It will be remembered also that during the twenty years intervening between the first edition of his work and the last one, his system received at his hands no modification or development worthy of note. It remained what it was at first, the initial product of a comparatively young man, who, by way of change, devoted himself for a short period to economic study. List's system, on the contrary, represents the labors of a professed economist, who for twenty years devoted himself earnestly to the study of economic phenomena, and to the construction of his economic system.

It is not, therefore, to be expected that Raymond's system should have received the same degree of development as did List's. But it is contended here that in Raymond's "Thoughts

---

[1] This refers to his second edition.

on Political Economy," published in 1820, and in his slightly
elaborated "Elements of Political Economy," published in
1823, are to be found enunciated the fundamental principles
that List takes as the basis for his "Outlines of American
Political Economy," 1827, and of his elaborated and more
complete work, "The National System of Political Economy," 1841.

A comparison of the works[1] of Raymond and of List will
show that the following fundamental theses are common to
both.[2]

*The dominant school of economists, Adam Smith and his
disciples, has not distinguished between private and public
economy, and has, therefore, treated of the economy of individuals rather than of political, or national economy.*

<table>
<tr><td align="center">LIST.</td><td align="center">RAYMOND.</td></tr>
<tr><td>"The component parts of po-
litical economy are, individual
economy, national economy,
and the economy of mankind."</td><td>"As national wealth is a dis-
tinct thing from individual
wealth, so political economy is a
distinct thing from private econ-
omy." P. 406.</td></tr>
<tr><td>"Adam Smith treats of the
economy of mankind and for-
gets to treat of the wealth of</td><td>"The fundamental error, as I
apprehend, into which Adam
Smith and most other writers</td></tr>
</table>

---

[1] Unless otherwise stated, the references by pages in the parallel
quotations are to Raymond's Elements of Political Economy, 1823,
and to Lloyd's translation of "The National System of Political
Economy," London, 1885. The references to "letters" of List
are to the letters that make up his "Outlines of American Political
Economy," Phila., 1827.

[2] Despite a specious appearance of method and logical arrangement
List's work is rambling and diffuse; and Raymond is prolix to a
degree, and hopelessly wanting in a methodical development of his
system. A brief comparison of their two systems is, consequently,
difficult, and bound to be more or less unsatisfactory. An attempt is
made in what follows to present in concise theses the fundamental
principles that underlie List's system, and in something like the
order of his development of them, and to show the similarity of
Raymond's theories by selected extracts bearing upon the same
points.

nations. . . . . "his book is a mere treatise on the question of how the economy of individuals and of mankind would stand, if the human race were not separated into nations, but united by a general law and by an equal culture of mind." Letter 1.

have fallen, ..., is their not having distinguished between public and private wealth." P. 155.

"Instead of treating of public economy they in fact treat of private economy; instead of talking about nations they talk about individuals." P. 139.

"We must be careful to keep in mind the distinct notion of a nation itself, and not confound it with. the individuals or any portion of the individuals of which that nation is composed; a thing that is often done by the best writers on political economy. It is, indeed, the prevailing error of every writer on the subject I have read. Whilst they profess to treat of national interests, they depart from the subject and treat of individual interests." P. 34.

"M. Say's work is liable to the objection of being a partial instead of a general treatise on political economy. It treats rather of private than of public wealth." P. 173.

The school of Adam Smith further fails to distinguish the interests of a nation from the general interests of the race, and its doctrines are therefore too cosmopolitical to admit of application in present actual conditions.

List.	Raymond.
"If the whole globe were united by a union like the twenty-four States of North America, free trade would be quite as natural and as beneficial as it is now in the Union."	"If governments could be administered upon the perfect principles of universal philanthropy, perhaps a nation might be required to forego an advantage to itself, upon the ground that the interests of other nations required it, although even
"There would be no reason for separating the interest of a	

certain space of land and of a certain number of human beings from the interests of the whole globe and the whole race . . . .

"There would be no national interest. . . .

"This state of things may be very desirable,—it may do honor to the heart of a philosopher to wish for it,—it may even lie in the great plan of Providence to accomplish it in after ages. But it is not the state of the actual world.

"Adam Smith's system, *in the world's present condition*, goes therefore along with the good Abbe St. Pierre's dreams of eternal peace, with the systems of those who fancy the laws of nations." Let. I.

"Cosmopolitan institutions . . . . are not yet ripe for being introduced into practice." Let. II.

then it would be doubtful; for those principles, by such expansion, become so dissipated, as to have no efficacy or power, and the old adage, 'charity begins at home,' is, no doubt, the best commentary that ever was written upon the doctrines of universal philanthropy.

"But at any rate, in the present state of the world, it would be chimerical to the last degree for a political economist to discuss the question, how far a nation should be governed in its policy towards other nations, by the principles of universal philanthropy. At present the duties of government extend no further than the protection of its own citizens, and the promotion of its own national wealth; and any chimerical notions of universal philanthropy, which carry the duty of a government to the superintendence, or consideration even, of the interests to the citizens of a foreign country are as unwise as they are impracticable." P. 166, V. II.

The school of Adam Smith assumes that the interests of the individual and of society are identical; that the individual best knows his own interests, and, if allowed to pursue his own interests in his own way, will necessarily further the interests of society. But this assumption is without warrant; the immediate interests of the individual and of society are often at variance; aud the temporary interests of the individual seldom ever harmonize with the permanent interests of society.

LIST.	RAYMOND.
" 'What is prudence in the conduct of every private family,' says Adam Smith, 'can scarcely	"It seems to be an admitted dogma with Doctor Smith that national and individual interests

be folly in that of a great king-dom.' Every individual in pursuing his own interests necessarily promotes thereby also the interests of the community. It is evident that every individual inasmuch as he knows his own local circumstances best and pays most attention to his occupation, is far better able to judge' than the statesman or legislator how his capital can most profitably be employed." P. 162.

"Is the wisdom of private economy also wisdom in national economy? Is it in the nature of individuals to take into consideration the wants of future centuries, as those concern the nature of the nation and the State? Let us consider only the beginning of an American town; every individual left to himself would care merely for his own wants, or at most for those of his nearest successors, whereas all individuals united in one community provide for the convenience and the wants of the most distant generations; they subject the present generation for this object to privations and sacrifices which no reasonable person could expect from individuals." P. 165.

"Nor does the individual merely by understanding his own interests best, and by striving to further them, if left to his own devices, always further the interests of the community. We ask those who occupy the benches of justice, whether they do not have to send individuals to the tread-mill on account of

are never opposed, but a more unsound doctrine in principle, or a more abominable one in its consequences can not well be imagined." P. 215, V. II.

"Public and private interests are often directly at variance." P. 220.

"Private citizens can only be expected to be wise for themselves—it is not their duty to look after the public interests—they are not the conservators of national wealth. This belongs to the department of legislation. If, from particular circumstances, . . . one species of industry is more profitable than another, it must be expected that individuals will embark in it, without any regard to the evil consequences it may produce to succeeding generations; but it does not become a legislator, either to be blind to their consequences, or not to guard against them. . . . No man can be expected to forego a present advantage to himself, provided there is no immorality in the enjoyment of it, upon the ground that it may be prejudicial to posterity. He may have no posterity, or if he has, their interests at the distance of two or three generations, are too remote to influence his conduct. The influence of self-interest on human conduct, like the laws of gravitation, is in the inverse compound ratio of distance and quantity.

"Legislators, however, are not permitted to take such limited short-sighted views of things, .

their excess of inventive power and of their all too great industry. Robbers, thieves, smugglers and cheats know their own local and personal circumstances and conditions extremely well, and pay the most active attention to their business; but it by no means follows therefrom that society is in the best condition where such individuals are least restrained in the exercise of their private industry. In a thousand cases the power of the State is compelled to impose restrictions on private industry. It prevents the shipowner from taking on board slaves on the west coast of Africa, and taking them over *t⌐* America." P. 166.

. . . . . they are traitors to their high trust, if they do not look to the future as well as to the present. Even according to the laws of self-interest, the remoteness of the interests of future generations, should be counterbalanced by the magnitude of those interests." P. 222.

"As a general rule individuals understand the management of their own affairs and the art of getting rich better than any philosopher can teach them." P. 156.

"An individual may study his own advantage by smuggling goods, but it will hardly be pretended that that is 'an employment most advantageous to the society,' or nation. An individual may study his own private advantage by employing his capital in the slave trade, but he would not thereby study the advantage of the nation." P. 214, V. II.

A true system of political economy cannot ignore the existence of separate nations.

Each nation is to be regarded as an organic unity; imperishable; having national interests separate and distinct from; often opposed to; and always paramount to, the private interests of individual citizens on the one hand, and to the interests of other nations, or of the race in general, on the other.

List.	Raymond.
"We have proved historically that the unity of the nation forms the fundamental condition	"A nation is as much a unity as an individual, and must always be so considered, when

of lasting national prosperity;

and we have shown that only where the interest of individuals has been subordinated to those of the nation, and where successive generations have striven for one and the same object,· the nations have been brought to harmonious development of their productive powers, and how little private industry can prosper without the united efforts both of the individuals who are living at the time, and of successive generations directed to one common object . ." P. 163.

"A nation is . . . a separate society of individuals,who,

possessing common government, common laws, rights, institutions, interests, common history and glory, common defense and security of their rights, riches and lives, constitute one body, free and independent,

following only the dictates of its interests, as regards other independent bodies, and

possessing power to regulate the interests of the individuals constituting that body, in order to˙ create the greatest quantity of

treating of national interests." P. 44.

"A nation is one, and indivisible; and every true system of political economy must be built upon this idea, as its fundamental principle." P. 44.

"When (public and private interests are) at variance, it is not to be made a question which ought to prevail." P. 220.

"What is true as it respects the duty of government, in regard to the slave trade so far as national interests alone are concerned, is true of every other measure relating to national industry, which has a remote tendency to affect national wealth and prosperity. The true policy for every wise legislator is, to consider the nation immortal, and to legislate for it, as though it was to exist forever." P. 224.

"A nation is an artificial being or a legal entity, composed of millions of natural beings." P. 35.

"A nation is a unity, and possesses all the properties of unity. It possesses a unity of rights, a unity of interests and a unity of possessions." P. 35.

"Every nation is to consult its own interests exclusively, without any regard to the interests of other nations. P. 166, V. II.

"The internal policy of a nation, ... should be modeled with a view to the general good. The welfare of the many common welfare in the interior, and the greatest quantity of security as regards other nations." Let. II.

"As individual liberty is in general a good thing so long only as it does not run counter to the interests of society, so is it reasonable to hold that private interests can only lay claim to unrestrained action so long as the latter consists with the wellbeing of the nation. But whenever the enterprise and activity of individuals does not suffice for this purpose, or in any case where these might become injurious to the nation, there does private industry rightly require support from the whole power of the nation, then ought it for. the sake of its own interests to submit to legal restrictions." P. 172.

"The State is not merely justified in imposing, but bound to impose certain regulations and restrictions upon commerce, (which is in itself harmless) for the best interests of the nation.", P. 167.

should never be sacrificed to that of the few." P. 166, V. II.

"The citizens should have as much liberty as is consistent with the good of the nation. To deprive him of this would be a tyranny. More than this he ought not to claim." P. 202, V. II.

"No citizen should have a right or an interest opposed to the general good of the nation." P. 201, V. II.

"The question whether individuals should be permitted to sell, where they can sell *dearest*, and buy where they can buy *cheapest*, ought not to be decided upon the narrow, contemptible principles of private interests, but upon the more expanded and noble precepts of public interests." P. 220.

"It is ever to be remembered trat the public interests are paramount to individual interests— that a private mischief or inconvenience must be endured for the public good; and that when a political economist has shown that public and private interests are opposed, he has made out a case in which the interposition of the government is necessary —he cannot be required to prove that private interests ought to give way—that is to be taken for granted." P. 201, V. II.

In contradistinction, therefore, to private or individual economy, and to cosmopolitical economy, or the economy of mankind, there is a national economy, arising out of the fact of the existence of separate nations.

Each nation, according to its circumstances, has its own particular system of national economy; and it is the province of a national economy to point out the means by which a nation may raise itself to the highest point of national prosperity and power.

<table>
<tr><td>LIST.</td><td>RAYMOND.</td></tr>
</table>

LIST.

"To complete the science, we must add the principles of national economy. The idea of national economy arises with the idea of nations." Let. II.

"National economy teaches how a certain nation in her particular situation may direct and regulate the economy of individuals, and restrict the economy of mankind; *i. e.*, how, in the absence of a lawful state including the whole earth, to create a world in itself, in order to grow in power and wealth, to be one of the most powerful, wealthy, and perfect nations of the earth." Let. II.

"In political economy there must be as much politics as economy." Let. II.

RAYMOND.

"Foreign theories and systems of political economy, from the dissimilarity in the nature of the governments, are altogether unsuited to our country." P. 5, 1st ed.

"Political economy is a science which teaches the nature of public or national wealth. . . . . It professes to teach the most effectual means of promoting a nation's wealth and happiness, and it embraces every subject which has a tendency to promote them." P. 9.

"It belongs to the department of the political economist to ascertain the operation of political institutions, and when they are found defective, or prejudicial, to point out the proper remedy. His immediate object should be to instruct governments how to legislate, and not individuals how to get rich." P. 150.

The system of Adam Smith and his school is a theory of exchange values, and these are the proper subject matter of individual economy.

National wealth consists, not in exchangeable commodities, but in productive powers; and therefore a national economy has little concern with values; it is concerned with the study of the development of productive power.

LIST.

"That Smith's school teaches nothing else than the theory of values, is seen not only from

RAYMOND.

"Another of the evil consequences of not distinguishing between public and private

the fact that it bases its doctrine
everywhere on the conception
of 'value in exchange,' but also;
from the definition it gives of
its doctrine. It is (says J. B.
Say) that science which teaches
how riches, or exchangeable
values, are produced, distributed
and consumed. This is un-
doubtedly not the science which
teaches how the *productive powers* are awakened and developed,
and how they become depressed
and destroyed." P. 138.

"Adam Smith's system is
nothing more than a theory of
values; a mere shopkeeper's or
individual merchant's theory—
not a scientific doctrine showing
how the productive powers of
an entire nation can be called into existence, increased, maintained and preserved,—for the
special benefit of its civilization,
welfare, might, continuance and
independence.

"This system regards everything from the shopkeepers'
point of view. The value of
anything is wealth, according to
it, so its sole object is to gain
values." P. 350.

"In individual and cosmopolitical economy the object is to
gain matter in exchanging matter for matter, as in the trade
of a merchant." Let. II.

"We must say to M. Jean Bap-
tiste Say at the outset that *political* economy is not, in our
opinion, that science which
teaches only how values in exchange are produced by individuals, distributed among them
and consumed by them; we say

wealth, is a constant liability to
mistake the proper subjects
which belong to the science.
Hence the tedious length to
which most writers have inves-
tigated the subject of value, and
the causes of its fluctuations,
supposing it to be the measure
of public as well as of private
wealth." P. 181.

"It is very natural for mer-
chants, when they turn politi-
cians, to use their own terms
and tools of art, . . . , but it
is the business of a political philosopher not to be misled by
these misapplications of terms,
nor to misapply them himself,
. . . and when treating of national wealth in gross, let him
·not use terms applicable to only
a part of the nation, and wholly
irrelevant and unmeaning when
applied to the whole nation." P.
296.

"*value* has very little application to public wealth, . . .
Property is the only subject of
value, and as property alone,
constitutes individual wealth,
those writers who confound national and individual wealth have
attached very great importance
to the word value, and have displayed a great deal of ingenuity
and talents in investigating its
nature and cause, and in endeavoring to fix upon its true standard." P. 56.

"If there be no distinction between national and individual
wealth, ... a treatise
on national wealth will be a treatise on individual wealth, *et e
converso.* This is degrading the

to him that a statesman will know and must know, over and above that, how the productive power of a whole *nation* can be awakened, increased and protected, and how on the other hand they are weakened, laid to sleep, or utterly destroyed; . . . ." P. 356.

"The prosperity of a nation is not, as Say believes, greater in the proportion in which it has amassed more wealth (*i. e.*, values of exchange), but in the proportion in which it has more developed its powers of production." P. 144.

dignity of the science of political economy into a paltry science of dollars and cents! Upon this supposition, it becomes the business of the political economist to teach individuals how to get rich, instead of teaching legislators how to legislate." P. 156.

"the comparative wealth of different nations will always depend upon the extent of this capacity. If one nation in proportion to its population, possesses a greater capacity for acquiring the necessaries and comforts of life than another, it possesses a greater share of national wealth." P. 48.

"So, if one nation has made greater improvements in the arts of sciences and in agriculture; if its lands are in a higher state of cultivation, if its roads, bridges, canals, mills, buildings and improvements are in a greater state of perfection than those of another nation, it has for all these reasons a greater capacity for acquiring the necessities and comforts of life, and therefore possesses a greater stock of national wealth." P. 50.

Raymond and List, alike, reject the economic system of the school of Adam Smith, on the ground that it is individual economy, not public, or *political*, economy; they both specifically deny the assumed harmony of interests between the individual and society; they both insist on the recognition of nations as organic unities; they both make *political* economy the science which regards the interest of the nation, as such, rather than the interest of the individual or the race;

they both reject *value*, denying it any place in a true theory of *political* economy; they both make national wealth to consist, not in commodities, as does private wealth, but in "capacity," or "productive power;" they both accordingly reject Smith's classification of productive and unproductive labor; they both reject his arguments for the international division of labor and free trade; they both advocate, in opposition to this, the harmonious development in each nation of agricultural and manufacturing interests; and they both repudiate *laissez faire*, and look to the government to conserve and develop national wealth.

This seems a rather unusual number of *coincidences* of thought, yet in themselves they are not sufficient to warrant the conclusion that List took his ideas bodily from Raymond. List himself says he was largely influenced in his conclusions by his study of American conditions;[1] and it is, of course, entirely possible that from a study of the same phenomena they were both led to the same ideas. The coincidences here noted are, however, sufficient to sustain the contention that Raymond at least anticipated List in the essential features of his system; and there are other circumstances which so strongly suggest the possibility that List was an unacknowledged debtor to Raymond, that to harbor the suspicion hardly exposes one to the charge of rash judgment.

In his American letters List hints at the genesis of his ideas, and in the preface to the first edition of his "National System," he goes into more detail of the history of his mental development in the matter of political economy. In this preface he states that as early as 1818 he "was not satisfied with teaching young men that science (political economy) in its present form;"[2] he had begun to entertain "doubts as to the truths of the prevailing theory of political economy."[3] Though at that time free trade seemed to him "accordant

---

[1] "The National System," p. 29.
[2] *Ibid.*, p. 25.
[3] *Ibid.*

with common sense, and also to be proved by experience," as seen in France and Great Britain, yet he saw in "the wonderfully favorable effects of Napoleon's continental system, and the destructive results of its abolition," things that seemed to him to be directly contrary to what he had previously observed. Then it was that the idea of "*the nature of nationality*" came tó him and "he perceived the distinction between *cosmopolitical and political* economy." In 1819 he was adviser of the German commercial league, and was waging a newspaper war with "an innumerable army of correspondents and leader writers, from Hamburg and Bremen, from Leipzig and Frankfort, and of this experience he writes: "In the course of the daily controversy which I had to conduct, I was led to perceive the distinction between the *theory of values* and the *theory of the powers of production.*" Such is the genesis of List's system, according to his own testimony.

In List's collected works, edited by Professor Häusser,[1] there are only five articles from his pen dated prior to his departure for America, and these all belong to the years 1819-20. In these there are no symptoms of that loss of faith in the doctrines of Adam Smith, which List avers had taken place as early as this date; much less is there any shadowing forth of the principles and the system he so distinctly enunciated soon after his arrival in the United States. Even his "Outlines," published in this country in 1827, hardly show such an advanced stage of development as he claims to have reached before he had left Germany; and so far as appears from Professor Hausser's collection, the "Outlines" are less a development than a complete contradiction of all that List had held and taught before. In view of this, one would hardly expect to find in the articles List wrote for the press during his newspaper controversy with the "innumerable army of correspondents and leader writers" much trace of

---

[1] "Friederich List's gesammelte Schriften, herausgegeben von Ludwig Häusser." Stuttgart and Tübungen, 1850.

what is so conspicuously absent in his more carefully prepared writings of that time.   But without consulting these one would perhaps not be warranted in stating authoritatively that no trace of List's new system can be found in his writings before his arrival in the United States.   These writings are not available to me, and in the absence of them I have to rest my conclusion on the authority of those who have made a study of the development of List's system, and who have been in a position to consult all of his writings.

Their testimony does not bear out List's statements as to when he first separated from the school of Adam Smith.   His recollection in 1841 of his mental development of twenty years earlier does not harmonize with Professor Leser's notion of that development as evidenced in List's writings.   In 1819 he was, according to Leser,[1] still dominated by the free trade principle of Adam Smith, and the only exception to it which he justified was by way of *retaliation;* and he regarded it as heresy to believe that internal industry could be awakened by customs duties.   In 1820 he is still insisting on the stock argument that a protective tariff only operates to divert industrial energy into lines for which a country was not fitted by nature, and thus to retard the development of the industries for which nature had particularly adapted the country; free trade was still the true system through which alone the highest degree of welfare was to be attained.   He showed himself still a true disciple of Adam Smith, and urged

---

[1]"Die Aufgabe, die ihm gestellt war, erfüllte er in einem Geiste der sich vollständig von der freihandelerischen Theorie der Engländer beherrscht zeigte.   Nicht auf die Begründung eines Deutschen Grenzzollsystems, sondern auf die Beseitigung der bestehenden Binnenzölle ist der Nachdruck gelegt; ja, nur von dem auch durch Adam Smith für berechtigt erklärten standpunkt der Retorsion wird überhaupt ein Zollsystem vertheidigt.   Dagegen bezeichnet es L. als eine notorische Irrlehre, dass die inländische Industrie durch Zölle geweckt werden könne."   Allgemeine Deutsche Biographie, p. 762.

that the welfare of the nation was impeded and destroyed in the same way as was that of individuals.[1]

At the very time when List claims already to have "perceived the distinction between cosmopolitical and political economy," and to have conceived his "theory of the productive powers," as opposed to the "theory of values," Prof. Leser stoutly maintains that he was still a loyal disciple of the school of Adam Smith, and engaged in defending its cosmopolitical principle of free trade.

Not only do List's "collected writings" bear out Leser in the contention that in 1820 List was still of the school of Smith, but this claim is further sustained by the fact that as late as 1822, when in exile in Strasburg, List proposed translating J. B. Say into German,[2]—a piece of work we should hardly look for in one so thoroughly out of sympathy with that author as List represents himself to have been.

Leser first finds List in opposition to the school of Smith in his "Outlines," published two years after his arrival in America; and he attributes this change of heart to the exigencies of List's new surroundings, and suggests that he found the materials for his new system ready to hand in the

---

[1]Von den Schutzzöllen wird geurtheilt, dass sie zu 'Productionen zwingen, welche der Natur des Landes, zu dessen Vortheil der Zwang Statt findet, nicht angemessen sind, und diejenigen beschränken, welche seine Natur entsprechen.' Die Wirkungen des Mercantilsystems werden als traurige bezeichnet; dagegen heisst die Welthandelsfreiheit ein Ideal, "wodurch einzig nur die höchste Stufe menschlichen Wohlstandes erreichbar scheint.' Auch in andern Punkten zeigt sich der Verfasser der Denkschrift als treuer Schüler des Smith'schen Systems. Er legt auf die Bilanz zwischen Production und Konsum grosses Gewicht; es legt die Vermehrung der Ausfuhr mehr Bedeutung bei als der Verhinderung der Einfuhr und erklärt, dass der Wohlstand der Nationen auf demselben Wege behindert und geschädigt werde wie derjenige der Einzelnen." *Ibid.*, p. 763.

[2]"Da wurden Plane gemacht zu grosseren literarischen Arbeiten; Say's Nationalokonomie sollte übersetzt und erlautert herausgegeben werden." Häusser, gesammelte Schriften, p. 178.

arguments then common in the United States.[1] It was in the air, so to say, and List only caught and gave a local habitation and a scientific name to what up to that time had been floating about in a vague way in popular discussion. The testimony of Eheberg—whose acquaintance with the writings of List is thorough—is also to the effect that List is found in opposition to the school of Adam Smith for the first time after his arrival in America;[2] and that he found his

---

[1]"L. blieb seiner Vergangenheit darin treu, dass er sich wiederum auf die Seite der strembsamsten und erwerbthätigsten Klassen stellte. Freilich handelte es sich nun nicht darum, wie in Deutschland Beschränkungen des inneren Verkehrs entgegenzutreten, sondern die industrielle Bevölkerung verlangte im Gegentheil Abschliessung vom Ausland durch hohe Sätze des Zolltarifs. Diese Bestrebungen waren natürlich mit der Smith'schen Theorie, in deren Geist seine früheren Argumentationen im Wesentlichen gehalten waren, nicht zu vertheidigen. Allein ihm blieb stets die Wissenschaft den Practischen Interessen untergeordnet, und er besass Belesenheit genug in neuern Staatswissenschaftlichen Schriften, um auch mit dem Gedankenreis der Schutzzöllner, wie sie namentlich in Frankreich und in Amerika selbst aufgetreten waren, bekannt zu sein. So vermochte er zur Unterstützung der Pennsylvanischen Industriellen theoretische Erörterungen zu veröffentlichen, deren hauptgegenstand die Bekämpfung der berühmtesten volkswirthschaftlichen Schriftstellers bildete." *Allg. Deut. Biog., p. 765.*
"Aber auch diese Ausführungen, die der nur mit Englischen Litteratur Bekannte für ganz originell halten mag, mochten den Amerikanern nur als eine blosse systematische Formulirung von Sätzen und Anschauungen erschienen denen sie in den Verhandlungen ihrer politischen Körperschaften und in den Aussprüchen hervorragender Staatsmänner schon begegnet waren." *Ibid.,* p. 766.
[2]Während List vor seiner Reise nach America sich im allgemeinen als Anhänger der Englischen Nationalökonomie giebt, stellt er sich in Amerika, anknüpfend an thatsächliche Verhältnisse, zum erstenmal der Adam Smith'schen Richtung entgegen, indem er der Freihandelstheorie die berechtigung des Schutzzollers entgegenhällt. Schon in den Amerikanischen Broschüren finden sich einige der seitdem oft gebrauchten Argumente zu gunsten der Schutzzolle, findet sich ferner die Betoning der wirthschaftlichen Bedeutung der nationen gegenüber dem Individualismus und Kosmopolitismus von Adam Smith, finden sich die ersten Anfänge sei-

theory ready to hand in the current arguments of the American protectionists.

It would seem then that List's system and Raymond's are, at bottom, practically identical; and that List conceived the idea of his system while a resident of the United States, and some years after Raymond's work had been given to the public. Is there any reason to believe that List was acquainted with Raymond's work? This is at least possible,—if not highly probable. In the absence of direct evidence on this point, we are left to conjecture from circumstances; and it is, in truth, harder to believe that List had no knowledge of Raymond's work than to believe that he was acquainted with it. Raymond's second edition had been given to the public less than two years before List's arrival in this country. It had not, it is true, had a wide circulation, nor commended itself to the popular reader; but it had received high praise,— even extravagant praise,—in many quarters, and had very much impressed some of the writers and thinkers of the day. It was highly thought of by men in Philadelphia, and was known to the press there. It had especially impressed Matthew Carey, who was prominent in the very organization for which List had prepared his "Outlines of American Political Economy," and who likely knew List. In his first letter in his "Outlines," List speaks as one who had been industriously delving into the literature of protection,[1] and mentions Niles' Register as one of the sources from which he had been

---

ner Lehre von den Productivkräften.   Auch die Benützung geschichlicher Thatsachen als Beweismittel zeigt sich schon hier. Die Besonderheit seiner Nationalokonomischen Auffassung erschient noch deutlicher in den in dem Jahren 1838 und 1840 veroffentlichten Artikeln; sie findet ihren beredlesten Ausdruk in dem Nationalen System der politischem Ökonomie.   Eheberg.   Handwörterbuch der Staatswissenschaften.   (1892).   P. 1056.

[1]"After having perused the different addresses of the Philadelphia Society for the Promotion of National Industry the different speeches delivered in Congress on that subject, Niles' Register, &c., &c., it would be but arrogance for me, &c."   Letter, July 10, 1827.

seeking to acquaint himself with protectionist doctrines. Had he gone back over a few numbers of the Register he would have found the announcement of the adoption of Raymond's work as the standard text book in the University of Virginia, for this item had appeared there just subsequent to the arrival of List in this country. List knew of Cooper's work, published in South Carolina, in 1826; and it seems, to say the least, "passing strange" that Raymond's work should so completely have escaped one who was attempting to acquaint himself with the literature of economics in America, who was doing this at the very time of the circulation of Raymond's book, and that too in the midst of men who not only knew, but admired the system enunciated in that book.

The sum of the whole matter, then, is this: that Raymond and List hit upon the same principles as the basis of their system of political economy; that Raymond had given his principles to the public some years before List had shown evidence of his having conceived similar ideas; and that List only gave his system to the world after he had had such opportunities for becoming acquainted with Raymond's work, that it is difficult to believe that he did not actually have a knowledge of it.

* 9 7 8 3 3 3 7 2 7 7 9 0 1 *